BUCK'S LAST WRECK

Selected Poems

David E. Thomas

Wild Variety Books
Missoula, Montana
1996

Wild Variety Books, a division of
Olsen's Publishing Co., Inc.
1013 Eaton Street
Missoula Montana 59801

ISBN 0-9649009-0-4
Library of Congress Catalog Card Number 95-61818

Cover art by Dirk Lee depicts the poet at rest on a friend's sofa.
Center art *Literary Missoula* by Jay Rummel depicts the poet and associates
in a popular niche of their urban habitat.

Book design by Peter Koch & Richard Seibert

DEDICATION

To My Parents, My Sister,
and My Brothers.

ACKNOWLEDGMENTS

Several of the poems in this book have been previously published. "Seasons In Prairie Blood" and "Fungus History" first appeared in *Montana Gothic* edited by Peter Koch. "The Ten Thousand Things" has perhaps the most extensive genealogy of any of my poems. It was first published in *The Borrowed Times*, then Scott Brady of *Cache Review* in Tucson showed me some points that needed revision and that led to the current configuration which appeared in the anthology *The Last Best Place*, edited by Bill Kittredge and Annick Smith. It also appeared in a Montana Historical Society publication "Work and Technology" and as a broadside in Peter Koch's series "Hormone Derange". "The Headwaters of the Marias" first appeared in one of Paul Piper's publications *Multiples* 7, as well as *The Last Best Place*. "How Things Went All Day" first saw print in *Northern Lights* during Dan Whipple's tenure as editor. "Industrial Meditation" appeared in the *All Montana Catalog* edited by Barbara Tucker. "Santos Going Fishing" I excerpted from my book *Fossil Fuel*. Dan Struckman printed "Out and About" in his magazine *Portable Wall*. "The Roxy" has become part of a local storytelling project on KUFM directed by Dana McMurray and others. "Historical Eggs In the Oxford Cafe" first appeared in Frank Ponikvar's *Missoula Comix* and then later Steve Smith included it in his book, *The Ox, Profile of a Legendary Montana Saloon*. David McCumber of *Big Sky Journal* published "Rough Morning" as a companion piece to a Jim Crumley article. "November Missoula Once More" was featured by Rick Newby in the Helena Film Society's *Front Row Center*. "Face To Face On Apgar" and "South of Chinook" appeared in *Camas* published by the

Environmental Studies Department of the University of Montana. And, finally, "A Night Without Sirens - Scalplock Lookout" was included in the anthology *More Than Animals* edited by Janet Pellam from Redtail Books in Pennsylvania.

There are enough people to whom I owe a debt of gratitude that to name them all would require a book several times the length of this little collection of poems so I am going to restrict myself to mentioning just a few who have had a direct influence on my literary efforts. Celeste Craig Sterritt who furnished me with the Smith-Corona portable typewriter I use to this day. Roger Dunsmore in whose Humanities seminars I first began writing steadily and who read every dreary word for years and still remains my friend. Ed Lahey who continually cheers me up and cheers me on. John and Judy Holbrook who keep the local fires well stoked. My old friend Peter Koch without whom this book would be impossible. Lance Olsen, his sister Lorie and κ2 without whom it would be inconceivable. Dirk Lee I thank for his cover and years of friendship in the day to day terrors of life as a Missoula artist. Jay Rummel has been my friend and teacher for a good twenty-five years and it's an honor to have his work included here. Bill Dolson taught me many things about style and purpose. Clint Long and the Andrus brothers, Al and Tom, contributed years of conversation and humor. Like I say, I could go on and on but space is limited so I'll thank Jim Crumley and Bill Kittredge for their very generous Forward and Afterward and be done with it.

David E. Thomas
23 March 1995 Missoula

CONTENTS

A REPORT FROM THE TOP RUNG

Jim Crumley

Dave Thomas is one of those people who make you feel better as soon as you see him. I've spotted his giant red beard and ponytail all over Missoula, identified his rolling working man's gait as he crosses the Higgins Avenue Bridge, and heard his warm chuckle, and started smiling even before my brain registered his presence. And I'm not the only one. All of the old Missoula hands feel the same way about Dave: as if he is the national treasure of our small, but extended nation, a nation founded on those sixties ideals of a love of language, a respect for hard work, friendships closer than blood, and a refusal to live by the bankrupt middle-class economic standards of greed and prejudice that had clearly destroyed America. With his poems and through his life Dave Thomas has been our saint, our ideal, the one of us who always knew the truth and was not afraid to speak it.

The first time I saw Dave Thomas, I probably didn't recognize him. It was the late sixties and I was teaching at the University of Montana. There was a lot of hair around campus in those days, but none of it on Dave Thomas's head. He had come from the small Hi-Line town of Chinook on an Army ROTC scholarship in 1965, so he was one of the less hirsute students. But by the time he stepped into my creative writing class in the spring of 1969, he had already begun wearing his trademark red flag of a beard. The first piece of fiction he turned in was a comic monologue of a story that Lenny Bruce would have been proud to have written. As teachers always know, I knew I had something here, had been presented with a talent that didn't need either my help or my guidance. This kid was going to go his own way, with or without me, and all I could do was convince him to rewrite it. Seven times is the number we remember. I didn't know then —— hell, nobody knew anything then —— that we were going to be buddies for nearly thirty years, or that Dave was going to create a body of poetry that marks him as the last and best of the hippie, working class, street smart poets.

Dave Thomas has spent those years actually working at the jobs that most of us gave up in our youth, working on the railroad as a tie gang laborer, worked construction as a laborer, demolition, clean-up, and wheeled endless barrows of concrete. Also, and obviously, he spent long hours writing in bars, on the roadside, and locked in small rooms all over the West working at his craft and art. And thus we have this body of work, poems about the dreary joys of manual labor, the warm comfort of old friends and fine conversation in home bars, the endless peace of Montana's various landscapes, and the lonely ecstasy of putting down the words, doing the work all alone.

Dave Thomas gives all of us hope that writing actually counts, that it makes life worth living, that the spirit endures, and as long as you can get that next word down on the page, you're living high, wide, and handsome.

Buck's Last Wreck

BUCK'S LAST WRECK

in memory of Tim O'Neill

reading
closer
than anyone
could tell
the fine print
of his
high speed
existence
beer foam
on prairie
    air
sagebrush eyes
scanning
gulleys
and benches
an explosion
of Milky Way
and Northern Lights
auto exhaust
shaped
his golden
Irish grin
scissor bill

          cap
      cockt
      to the wind
      passenger
      on his last
          ride
      feeling the ice
      no wheel
      to turn.

                    8 Dec 79
                    missoula

LEAVING KASLO

for Alice, the Warwicks, & D. Blouin

pristine waves of dark water
        hard snow
        peaks glint
        gold in sun
bird calls echo and woodpecker
          pounds his drum
spine and nerves recoil
      with silent shock   .
space is crowded with forest
      brush tangles
      passage
      to the white indifference
the cabin is strewn with Alice's
                 life
I pack my pack
    in nervous haste
the road's warm
      the day's clear
my thumb responds a ride
           or two
narrow mountain valley
     shoots me out
wide flat farmland south B.C.

marsh and river
smell
mountains further back
the relief of space
my prairie youth not yet
consumed.

April 1973

SEASONS IN PRAIRIE BLOOD

a slow wind rises out
    of sagebrush dust
    claims first light
across barbed wire

out of small cold shadows
    sheep rise
        a hungry baaing
and clanking of bells

the border collies know
        their job
nip the flock together
    on close cropped
        stubble

the solitary man
    in his round top
        wagon
gathers up his breakfast
        fire

the day is long against
    his empty mind
in town on hot streets

childhood games
are played in sparse shade
downtown money changes hands
signatures fixed
     decisions made
     in hot rooms
yes this place is on the map

mother orders groceries
     over the phone
and autumn leaves begin
     to fall

raked in piles they burn
     a pungent smoke
that stings young eyes
     makes blood run quick

dry cornstalks fill the garden
     pumpkin pie
     and haystacks
     red gold in setting sun

red-skinned girls dance
     their secret way
home to Moccasin Flats

diesel trucks roar thru town
    exotic exhaust fills
      the air with distant dreams
a freight whistle cuts thru
    suppertime
    and spinach grows cold
      on a fork

night sneaks up like a coyote
    prairie dogs dive
      in their holes
but the hot rod kids are just
    warming up chasing
      the highway patrol
    down hi-way 2

barrow pit beer bottles
    pop open with
    a church key twist
a religious whiff
    of cool dry air

tires hum thru radio static
    steering around
    gravel corners
    seeking high ground

the long distance big city
message
floats across the great
American Desert

crackling past prairie dogs
coyotes
nighthawks and
sheepherders

the latest hot sound
of neon dreams
blaring out open windows
in a beat up Ford

the Milky Way
arching a billion tiny
lights
over
a young drunk
pissing beer
on the shivering ground.

26 Aug 77
missoula

THE HEADWATERS OF THE MARIAS

"I walkd

all the way

to Rock City

from here

and took pictures

met an old boy

from Heart

Butte, said

this is heavy

spiritual

turf, taboo

to Indians…

pictures

never turnd

out." blank

frame no frame

at all

these sandstone

bluffs

cut by relentless

wind

and water

older

than any name

we lean

on a brand new

Ford pick-up

as Sweetgrass

speaks

and first

a white splash

in the Two

Medicine River

then a quick

dark leap

snaps a fish

clear

of the late

summer water

low and muddy

the fish

finds its tail

and disappears

in the evening light.

2 Aug 84
on the hi-line

HOW THINGS WENT ALL DAY

Irv came to work hung-over
they had been bowling
the night before
and of course they
drank and so he
was hung-over when
he went to get his
dump truck
and bring us a load
of dirt
for our backfill
the kid and I
stood watching him
and we didn't
notice anything
it was early
in the morning
and we were each
preoccupied
with our other
lives so we didn't
realize until he
hoisted the bed
of the dump
that it was

empty - the
tailgate banging
against
nothing but
the morning
air cool
and dusty.

28 Apr 1985
missoula

THE TEN THOUSAND THINGS

Well let's see there's
    shebolts hebolts and stress rods
there's make-up bolts inbed bolts and
        carriage bolts
there's nuts and washers to fit all sizes
    of each.
There's rattle guns 18
    and 24 inch
      crescent wrenches - spud
      wrenches
    and porto- power
      jacks.
There's double jacks and jack hammers
    pinking eyes and inbed plates.
There's Foreman Frank for whom
    I work
    and foreman Al and foreman
      Stan and foreman Rags
    the superintendent and his vice.
There's the dry shacks the print shack
    the fire barrels
the lumber stockpile. There's 2x4's
2x6's 2x12's 4x6's 1x2's
    1x4's 1x6's
    in all different lengths.
    There's the Safety Man and

"Access Closed"
signs there's roped off areas
and KEEP OUT
DANGER ABOVE signs.
there's water jugs on the cranes
and there's the nip truck
and its driver bringing in the
goods
nobody can find there's okum
and tie wire big rolls of tape
red plugs
and rock anchors
wing nuts
and cable clamps
not to mention cables and their
shackles
and turn-buckles.

There's the sky turning ever more purple
as the shift
swings toward
its end black by
lunch and stars
from then on mercury
vapor lamps and a
heavier coat.
there's pull ropes to the cans up concrete
columns

    there's catwalks
      and scaffolds
   There's times when I wander
     about picking up
     and sorting bolts
  there's times when a chance glance
      at a star
      trying to outshine
      the lamps
is all the rest I get. It happens every night
     from 4:30 pm
     to 12:30 am
     at Libby Dam.

Oh damn! I forgot nails! 16 common
     16 duplex 8's the same
     roofing nails and blue
         heads
    There's just no end to it

    Sorting bolts on the edge
     of artificial light
    the tune of an engine
     the shadow of the dam.

      28 Sept 1971
      libby montana

INDUSTRIAL MEDITATION

a dusty grove of Indians
and campesinos
waits for a truck ride:

deep in the concrete
steel glass cocoon
motor homes
slick as beetles
proceed nose to ass along
asphalt and concrete
laid out according to viral
suggestion
vibrating like Mayan
glyphs
in a child's dream
blind old Arizona cowboy tells
stories of 666
by a fruitpicker's
fire
entropic algebras of cultural digestion
yawn at daybreak
in a high mountain
village
from a four wheel drive
bearing a government sign

computer circuits whirr as language
after language
is reduced to a key punch
code
"coffee" "tobacco"
"coal" and "oil"
spells
the international countinghouse
culture
myths and handwoven designs
carrying centuries of human breath
and smell
fade into dacron polyester
automated factories shuffle

between jungle and dawn
a charcoal burner
plies his dying
trade
in a volcano's sleeping
fire
and on the streets of a Mexican town
a freckle faced
Indian woman is captured
by a loudspeaker her child
slung in a blanket

on her back
a flickering unfocused bone
pickt vulture clean
windy colors sprouting
new feathers
of life and death.

4 Feb 78
san cristobal
de las casas

NOCTURNAL ESCONDIDO

the rooster el gallo
plays a harsh
note
unconcerned for dawn
his understudy the turkey
will never make
first chair
cats sound like distressed
babes
crying out the night
myriad bird calls
donkey brays
rasp on washboard palms
but the final movement
is the drum
and bugle boys
at the fort down the way
they do a hi-school
football half-time number
until the sun
is definitely
at attention
diesel buses growl
early morning

Spanish floats
down the road
somebody always laughs
then us gringos
begin to stir.

for Al & Louise
16 Jan 78

SANTOS GOING FISHING

A portrait without paints
visions behind eyes
     the open sea
sharp empty air
warm this far south
     even now
       snow and cold
have captured the mountains
     of home
his face is round
     and quick
mouth full of rapid Spanish
skin brown
with ancestry and sun
         eyes
         flick
across waves
catching sign of fish
  perched on gunnel
  he hauls up lobster
     trap
bare feet like pelican claws
a stocky walk
over rock and sand
he cooks with ferocity

knows the power
     of his spices
his "maquina" runs on constant
care parts
are hard to find
his sierra line comes in fighting
     will his boat
     be full?

"Aiyee!!" he cries
     shakes his head
a greenhorn falls in his boat
he pours "l'alcohol" in his "cafe"
waits for supper by oil light
a cigarette
dangles straw hat
and sandals the portrait
          is never finished
of Santos going
fishing

14 Dec 74
chacala, nay, mex

revised: 17 Sept 92
missoula

FUNGUS HISTORY

a barroom dancer
moves a hot summer
wind
his toes etch Hopi
sand
his eyes

mushroom hieroglyphs
from cowshit
twisting boulevard trees
in a rebellion
of haunted pounding

ghostly streetlights
and neon signs
rise to an uncertain
moon

a strangled cry from the host
of spores
ungrateful tentacles
soak polish
from the barroom floor

as the dancer
whirls
his tribal blood
across
one shaky bridge
then another

following the strained scent
of damp earth
cutting across dawn
like a diamond
in the rough.

17 Aug 77
missoula

OUT AND ABOUT

Today all my shortcuts
are passable
the snow mostly high
on mountain
ridges
delightful to the eye
no impediment
to feet
the brush along the river
a raw tangle
as I pass by
the fresh green of new leaves
yet to heal
the harsh brown
of winter's frost
the gravel pit
that once was
the Fox Theatre
a sad reminder
of human design
today I am free
from the routines
of ordinary labor
and so wearing a coat too warm

for the sun
that has begun
to prevail
    I walk through town
    on a mission
    of perception
I know I'll miss
        something
        crucial
a broken twig
    a muddy track
an old cowboy movie
    playing across
        the changing
        sky.

March 1991
missoula

THE ROXY

A perfect blue sky
                    sun
warm for February
I walk
in the sparkling air
not a trace
of smoke anywhere
                    fifty years
stand
in a pile of ashes
        popcorn
        aromas
and overpriced sodas
the dank interior
the tattered screen
but the seats were
        comfortable
the price right
and time
eased away
in the dancing
                    light
that played
            every night

of those
fifty years
   yesterday
swallowed
in a tongue
   of flame
a wall of smoke
rising
to the tune
of Saturday night
and today
   blue sky
warm sun.

20 Feb 94
missoula

A TATTERED LUXURY

she's big and beautiful
dressed like
a rummage sale
queen
knows every aisle of Sally Ann
and Goodwill
like a floorwalker in Macy's
carries at all times
paste-on stars
to cover emergency
celebrations
swoons before pinball
geniuses
loves musicians
takes time to talk
with poets
and paints her own pictures
on Missoula's
dreary sidewalks
passing by
like a gypsy
on her way
to a ball
crystal clear she shines

a moon full
beyond waning
and the stars
   the stars . . .

for Alexis

29 Mar 77
missoula

HISTORICAL EGGS IN THE OXFORD CAFE

There was a time
        when women
would enter
only
on a dare
        a sorority gal's
meat and potatoes
sizzle
        a greasy grill
drunk
bleary faces move
thru
well lit smoke
wooden counter chairs
shine
with decades of hungry
asses
a freshman
from the University
        across the river
sips under age
1966 beer
a brand new deck
of cards flies

one
at a time
            calculating
            fingers
drum
a green felt table top
the dealer's shade
reflects
a row of chairs
against the back
            wall
tired flesh
a fading pension
spongy winos
the shoeshine boy
            snaps his rag
            all the way
to Mexico
and walls come
down the card games
                        divide
and multiply
a beehive hair-do
            plops
a cold foamy
            schooner

on a bloatd red
            nose
two fuzzy eyes
            can't
believe themselves
Mike Mansfield
            strides
thru in an old
            blue
suit greeting
gnarld ballot box
            faces
a divorcee
with two grandkids
            yells
"stretch one!"
from a printd card
second hand stretch
pants
bend to soapy dishes
the keno girl's
lipstick
shines like a neon
            sign
and a Greyhound bus
empties

ten thousand miles
along
a remodeld counter
wondering
what happend
to the cranky
old boys
who knew what
        the menu
        meant.

6 June 1979
missoula

EDDIE'S CLUB

Some nights we
were all so stoned
you could float
a battleship
       other
       times
it was just
a couple guys
       so hard
       and mean
you knew they
carried
the cold blue steel
       of the wrong
       side
       of life
As you came
in the front door
a candy counter
greeted you
but it gathered
       dust
       most
       traveled
further along
the mute

but shining mirror
and took
their place
amid the uproar
    Captain
    Light
would be holding
    forth
about dirigibles
and lightshow
while Shelhammer
hatched a scheme
    that
threatened to change
the world
Big D and Deschamps
squared off
for a gunfight
    that
would tune up
the night
and of course
there'd be
Jay Rummel just
in from San Francisco
to sing
the country blues
    now Crumley

we all remember
had an office
behind the cooler
where he wrote
    dark
    tales
that shadowed
the brightly burning
      lights
big-time dealers
appeared
in fancy cars
bought a round
    for the house
and glided
away
    Vic
and Satch
would drift
in from the Res
scouting
the return
of the Buffalo

We weaved
and warped
    each
    other

into a tapestry
of memory
Mortar fire and napalm
etched our nerves
some recoiled some
        dissented
many died, a lot just
watched on tv
but those of us who
        came
        to the bar
fought our war
as we saw it
we did not come
to knit and sew
    especially
    the girls
Gutowski, Eichwald
        Helding
McGehee walking
tables called
    every bluff
and those Salish
gals who loved
    "Green Onions"
while us knuckleheads
cheered the NFL
there's no end

to this saga
not the bare
squares
on the wall
nor the wax
of a used car lot
It meant
something
this old saloon
a place where
we lived
and died
and went
on to other things
but what
of the bartenders
the question remains
well
they lived
and died and went
on to other
things themselves

There 's a whole
dimension
missing here
the railroad
brakemen the carpenters

old Charlie Hall
       the retired
       redcap
faces Lee Nye recognized
       with his
       camera
Betty Reynolds
       with her
Charles Laughton
       face
and silver screen
       heart
called all the young
       longhaired
bearded guys
"Grandpa"
       while Adam
Gardipe stole
       thru the crowd
with a hot item
       or two
Jeff Wright the Fish
       Creek
packer observed
       the melee
with osprey wizened
       eyes
and Joe Malletere

rolled
his famous
cigarette perched
on a barstool like
a cutting horse
It was
a neighborhood
Gallagher
once said
playing guitar
and singing songs
from the Butte
copper mines
oh we had Mutt
and Jeff
and Captain Phil
and the Dope Patrol
the pay phone
played a role
and bad checks
bounced to death
but always
in the morning
the old men
got up to play
a quiet
game
of breath

against sunset
and
when some young
drifter
hauled in from
Mexico
they barely tipped
a nod

it was a neighborhood
this Eddie's Club
and it
can't end here

- for Reginald T.S. Loser
and Georgie Neva -

and in special
memory of Tony Piccinni
who owned the bar.

June '87
missoula

MONDAY MISSOULA

a brain
full of cartoons
walking all
over town
listening
to leaves fall
and autos cough
a slow blues
storms
roll over
the high ridges
snow
on Lolo Peak
glistens
like a fresh
    cake
late in the afternoon
the cartoons
come to life
Happy Hour
Top Hat Bar
  but more
  than that
  the story

keeps changing
       technicolor
       elbows
       sometimes I
       wish I woulda
       paid
       more attention
       high school
       physics
       what a drag
       real world
       real world
       technicolor
       necks
       scratchd
       with midnight
       paws.

14 Oct 1980

ROUGH MORNING

I can not count
    the spikes
I've pulled
    or driven
    the rails
I've seen laid
    across
    fresh
    adzed
ties
but when I approach
the Madison Street
    crossing
and meet
a freight slowly
    creaking
through my hung-over
    mind
I shudder
to resist
the temptation
    the desire
    to climb
the brakeman's ladder
the narrow
catwalk
above the coupling

and drop
to the other side
        as once
I'd've done
without a thought
        but now
I wait
until the last car
        passes
and on the other
side in an old brick
        house
crumbling
in its own sweet time
Sheila in her
        nightgown
waves
and smiles her beautiful
        Irish smile
as I pass
her window toward
        Charlie's Bar
and a hair
    of the dog
that bit me.

29 Aug 93
missoula

NOVEMBER MISSOULA ONCE MORE

First snow
   of the year
      blows
off the high ridges
   and
      sweeps
      down
      the streets
of town dusting
      windowsills
with a chill
that quickens
      blood
      beyond
      words
a necessity
of movement
      steam heat
      in small
      rooms
what
I need to find
      buzzes
      my ears

the last fly
of the year
a desperate
bug
fresh off the river
gone now
the scent
of winter strong
my nose
to the wind.

1988

GRANDPA ADAM GARDIPE

you slippt away
    in the night
a breath
between dreams
we all knew you
"Hey Rip, gimme a buck!"
Coyote's tariff
on a good time
you were his agent
turning solitary
        tragedies
into magic dances
fuelld by white port
and MD-20/20
you knew all the chemicals
of ecstasy
and sadness too –
"Adam, get up it's a nice
                day"
ah let me sleep I'm
an old man
and I seen lotta
        nice days
The White Buffalo
grazing
psychic pastures

behind Al's Bar
along Woody Street
and Front Street
goosing the girls
and soaking all
      comers
for a quarter
the price of a good
time slowly
eeking it's toll
"It is a good day
      to die
I am all scarrd up!"
cried one of Crazy
      Horse's
      warriors
you in the hospital
no longer answer
the call of the tubes
and the pumps
gone now on the star
      trail
gone
and gone.

24 Mar 1983
missoula

A CHANT FOR BEARS

in my small government
                    room
I dance the revenge
of all creatures who
cannot speak
in human terms
        who
do not drive large
        tin walld
            vehicles
over narrow asphalt
escaping the confines
of their lives
without success
desiring splendor
without danger
beauty without death
they cannot stand
grizzly bear claws
ripping the tents
        of their dreams
only large caliber
            magnum
            pistols
and bearproof garbage
cans

have reality in their world
but I dance
the ridge on Heaven's Peak
the relentless rise
of Huckleberry trail
the silence of doe eyes
and elk calves
stretching the road
for thick brush
I dance for this medicine
     country
the granite remains
of glacial waltzes
slow and more exact
than Mozart
I feel the cold
the heat wind
  and rain
all fools shall
pass away - me too
all that remains:
the sharp edge
of St. Nick
evaporating
another world

1981

FACE TO FACE ON APGAR

a nameless
terror grabs
me as I stand
with more
before my eyes
than I can
stand to see
a closeness
that threatens
my civilized
mind so used
to four walls
now this huge
circle
beyond my possible
self
a sky so blue
my name
is lost
peaks so jagged
I have no mind
I want
to escape
this voidness
the beauty
it holds

is more
than any word
The Ground
Squirrel Buddha
of this place
keeps an eye
on us all
I am nervous
from last night's
beer breakfast
coffee sex thoughts
beside the point
this wind
this wind!
keeps us
all alive
like a broken
down medicine
man I can hardly
stand
I must bow
to the Four Directions
and love
the wind

What?
this radio
antenna?

this lookout
shack?
the repeater
station with its
tower? These
things? Parkwide
communication: Mount
St. Nicholas
talks
to Mt. Brown
in cloud
language
the sun listens
like chlorophyll
coursing leafy veins
in a huckleberry
patch grizzly shit
on the switchback
trail.

8 June 1980
west glacier

HUCKLEBERRY LOOKOUT 4TH OF JULY 1981

there is no higher
            place
the Great Range
of the Rockies
etchd
against wisps
        of cloud
and blue sky
The Great Divide
a sparrow hawk
glides
in the wind
a bee buzzes
my hat
I am
with some friends
drinking whiskey
Peacock
makes chili
Lisa suns
    her pregnant
            self
Clark
sits and watches

Bob and Peter
are reading
the radio
burps
now and then

sometime later
Clark and I
look down
on an airplane

the clear cuts
and the raw
bends of the North
                    Fork

                    west glacier

A NIGHT WITHOUT SIRENS — SCALPLOCK LOOKOUT

for Peacock, Bauer, and Sullivan

wild creatures
long earred
    moon lit
snow hares
summer
dark sneak
into
half-baked
neon dreams
advertising
a wealth
of futility
beneath
the wheeling
    stars
a slow ache
of time
pounding
pounding
in the heart
of dawn
spreading
gold

and blue
　　　deep
and sweet
over raw
ridges
wordless
and serene.

15 July 1984

SOUTH OF CHINOOK

The Milk River crawls
   October low
a few leaves
  color
   cottonwood
    branches
ranchers
from the south
    country
rumble the bridge
there
is a breeze
and clouds float
   spare
across blue sky
it is good
to sit alone
away from town
  though
its sounds echo close by
I grew up
on this river
  my clumsy skates
knew its lumpy

ice
its chlorine
laced water
quenched my young thirst
the play
of its current
created
and devoured
my demons
the big old white house
with green fake shutters
has been sold
four days now
Dad
and I (Mom when able)
have been
sorting memories
and the objects
that evoke them
stick figure
drawings
early grammar lessons
photo upon photo
timorous
tenuous
ties to the past

strings
of Christmas lights
crumbled easter egg
       shells
candles
of humble ceremony
    packed
    for sale
finally the open air
calls me
the soft breeze
    the dance
of the Bear's Paw
    hidden
    in the cloud
and I walk
    to this river
    sand
where now I sit
the Milk crawls
    and cloud
briefly hides
the sun.

9 Oct 92

THE CORNER OF WOODY AND ALDER

for Rose

How tedious
  the merchant's
    life
counting buttons
  appraising
the worthless
   for the fool
while dust
   gathers
and history
    mourns
its better times
oh sweet nickel
   and lovely
    dime
what will
   this lace
    bring
against
the rotten lime
that once held
   these bricks
   so tight

love
and love alone
      so alone
holds the bitter
      wind
from the frail
      texture
of this enterprise.

October 87
missoula

DAVE THOMAS: THE USES OF POETRY

William Kittredge

On hot summer evenings long ago, when the door to Eddie's Club on Higgins Avenue in Missoula would be open to the street, and the last of the sunlight fell in long flat slants over the worn floorboards, reaching deep inside, to myself and people I knew at one of those rickety tables, I would settle both my hands around a fresh Cutty ditch and think, "This is it."

What I meant was not the booze, but companions all around and not a thing in the world to sweat, not right then, at that moment. It was like a childhood state of being; there would always be another morning; everything was forgivable; perhaps, like good babies, we actually were bulletproof and invisible.

But no. Some chemicals proved sort of toxic when we took them into our bodies in quantity; some behavior, while not exactly unforgivable, proved fatal, at least to any easy sense of well-being. Some friends are gone forever.

Which is partways why, these latter days as dark winter afternoons give way to early nightfall, the streetlights glowing orange and unreal before suppertime, I'm reassured when I see Dave Thomas hiking south across the Higgins Avenue bridge across the Clark Fork, heading for home. Some things have lasted. In Dave's words

it was a neighborhood

It still is. Dave's presence and his poems, his good grace and humor, remind us that these times, sweet and sometimes bitter, all day long, inescapably, are what we get to have, and that while they won't last forever, they can indeed be enough.

ABOUT THE AUTHOR

David E. Thomas was born and grew up on the Hi-Line in Northcentral Montana. Following his graduation from Chinook High School he entered the University of Montana where his life began to change in unexpected ways. Initially an enthusiastic ROTC cadet, he won a scholarship for his junior and senior years, but as the Vietnam War ground on and on his conscience demanded a shift in perspective and he found himself part of the psychedelic movement on the streets of San Francisco. There he became acquainted, through their work, with his immediate literary forebearers, Jack Kerouac, Gary Snyder, Richard Brautigan, Allen Ginsberg and many lesser lights prowling the Haight-Ashbury and North Beach in the late sixties and early seventies. Economic realities drove him to seek and find work, first on railroad gangs, but also on big construction projects like Libby Dam. He has also worked on a potato ranch, picked cherries on Flathead Lake and traveled extensively in the United States, Mexico and Central America with brief visits to Colombia and Ecuador. He currently lives in Missoula, Montana, eking out an existence as a janitor and odd job man while writing continuously.

21 March 1995

PUBLISHER'S NOTE

Dave Thomas keeps his poems flying pretty close to the ground. Whether it be the banging of an empty dump truck's gate, the sight of snow-capped peaks on a morning when shortcuts have become passable, or glacial waltzes slow and more exact than Mozart, Dave Thomas has been there, and has seen that, and has done that, and has written well about it. Dave is a storyteller, a teller of tales you can trust. And his tales range across a wide and varied world. This collection encompasses tales from Canada to Mexico, and observations ranging all the way from the details of day labor in the construction industry to the anatomy of souls tortured by morbid fear of grizzly bears. There are few poets anywhere so versatile as Dave. For too long, only a small circle of admirers have known his work. If this book helps to correct that problem, even if only a little, it will have been a success.

When my sister Lorie said that it seemed like it ought to be possible to get a collection of Dave's poems published somewhere, I thought well of course. This is it.

Dave selected this collection of poems, which is to say that he's the one to credit or blame for each and every choice. It just so happens that I endorse his choices, which is of course why Wild Variety Books is publishing the collection. This book is the first to come out under the Wild Variety Books label, and a book of Dave Thomas poetry seemed and still seems to me a thoroughly credible way to start a line of books. Thanks, Dave.

And thanks ever so much to Richard Seibert and Virginia Sulier for their indispensable help with the manuscript. Getting a manuscript headed toward becoming a book was a lot sweeter process because of the help you gave. Same for you, K2. Few publishers with partners are as lucky as Wild Variety was to have Kathleen Kimble as a partner in this venture. The rest of the thanks were taken care of in Dave's acknowledgements, at the front of the book.